SEASONING
FOR THE WORLD

SEASONING
FOR THE WORLD

FIRST EDITION

BRO. AUSTRA L. GALLOWAY

ADVICE AND GUIDANCE BY
REV. DR. TIMOTHY R. GREEN, JR.

XULON PRESS

Xulon Press
2301 Lucien Way #415
Maitland, FL 32751
407.339.4217
www.xulonpress.com

© 2021 by Bro. Austra L. Galloway

All rights reserved solely by the author. The author guarantees all contents are original and do not infringe upon the legal rights of any other person or work. No part of this book may be reproduced in any form without the permission of the author.

Due to the changing nature of the Internet, if there are any web addresses, links, or URLs included in this manuscript, these may have been altered and may no longer be accessible. The views and opinions shared in this book belong solely to the author and do not necessarily reflect those of the publisher. The publisher therefore disclaims responsibility for the views or opinions expressed within the work.

Unless otherwise indicated, Scripture quotations taken from the King James Version (KJV) – *public domain*.

Paperback ISBN-13: 978-1-6628-2048-9

Ebook ISBN-13: 978-1-6628-2049-6

DEDICATION

Lee Galloway my grandfather and **Sam Galloway** my father said something that became a part of my daily life. Sometime he would give me a task that was a very difficult task for me. I informed him that the task was too difficult. He would reply. 'You are not holding your mouth right.' I ask him what my mouth had to do with me taking a rusty nut of a rusty bolt? He would reply, "I didn't hear you ask the Lord for help with the problem with your mouth." So, I ask the Lord for help and it came to me that I should put some oil on it. By the way I was about ten or twelve years at that time. I learn at an early age to depend on the Lord for everything.

Table of Contents

Preface ix
Introduction xi

Chapter 1: Salt 1
Chapter 2: Grandpa Said 13
Chapter 3: Grandma Said 21
Chapter 4: Build on Your Vision 29
Chapter 5: Bully medicine and focus 37
Chapter 6: Sign of the Times 47
Chapter 7: This is the way 57

PREFACE

This book is a synopsis about the religious side of my upbringing. My great-grandparents were slaves (1865 era), and my grandparents were born at the end of slavery. The only thing that brought them through the hard times was the Almighty God. I was raised on a farm with my grandparents because my mother passed away when I was six months old. My father's parents raised my sister and me.

My grandparents were blessed and received forty acres and two mules from the government; however, it was not free. As a farm boy, I learned a lot about work ethics. *Early to bed, early to rise, makes a man healthy, wealthy, and wise.* I learned to have faith in God and myself.

I got to know God personally when I was twelve years old. Then, I saw all the marvelous and wonderful things God did while I was working with my grandfather. Afterwards, and throughout my life, I saw the need for a book like this to help everyone put a cutting edge on their faith, learning what God has done and what He can do for each of us. All we must do is believe in Him and have faith in God and yourself.

INTRODUCTION

This book is designed to provide a convenient repository of important spiritual facts. This is not a book of logic, but rather of facts concerning the role of someone raising the spiritual awareness of what God said He would do if we would serve Him.

Each chapter contains important significant emotional events. The solutions for some of the events are found in the pages of this book. Such information provided can be valuable to the young, old and to students at all levels, and is also good for general readers. The spiritual enlightening in the pages of this book in some degree will be the bedrock for a springboard to spiritual growth.

So, while you read through the pages of this book, remember this is not fiction; it is a true story. Every time you read this book, you will come to a different conclusion and/or answer to your situation based on your spiritual condition. I am honored to serve our country again by sharing how developing your relationship development with The Almighty God can be great for you. I am honored that our Lord has allowed me to share the heartbeat of my faith. The information in this book will allow you (or give you) the opportunity to look at life through life's prism and you will see many of life's paths, both spiritual and physical. Reading this book time after time you will heighten your level of wisdom and understanding.

CONTRIBUTORS

SEASONING FOR THE WORLD

Advice and guidance	Rev. Dr. Timothy R. Green, Jr.
Author	Bro. Austra L. Galloway
Reference	King James version Study Bible

Salt

CHAPTER 1

SALT

SALT I

Mr. J. L. is a beloved Sunday School teacher, a deacon, and a treasurer at Christian Light Missionary Baptist Church in Metcalfe, Mississippi in the early- to mid-sixties. This was a small town consisting mostly of black farmers, a town where ninety percent of the people went to church and Sunday School on Sunday.

Mr. J. L. had some children, and after a hard day's work he would sometimes sit on his wooden bench near the woodpile and have a little Bible study with his children. The neighbors, seeing him doing this, would send their children, because they knew that they would get some good spiritual information. Mr. J. L. would see them coming and wait for them. When they got there, he would start the session with a prayer for them, starting with the Lord's Prayer (Matthew 6:9–13). Then, he would thank God for keeping them safe and ask God to watch over them.

Speaking to the children after the prayer, Mr. J.L. said, "Good evening, you all."

The children, Lewis, Thickpin, and Charlie said all together, "Good evening, Mr. J.L."

Lewis was eleven years old, the shortest of them all, with high energy, always busy trying to learn or do something. Thickpin was somewhat chubby and wanted to be a farmer. Charlie always had a trick up his sleeve that would make you laugh. At twelve years old, Charlie was the oldest.

Mr. J. L. said, "This evening, we are going to talk about one of the main ingredients of food and compare the name of this ingredient in a spiritual sense to our spiritual lives. Years ago, before everyone could afford cold storage, salt was used to preserve meats and other products because of its composition. Salt preserves and cures, plus it inhibits the growth of microorganisms by drawing water out of microbial cells through osmosis. Bactria, fungus, and pathogens cannot survive in a salt environment.

Mr. J.L. continued, "In a spiritual sense, you are the salt of the earth; but, if a salt has lost its savor, wherewith shall it be salt?" *(Matthew 5:13)*.

Lewis asked, "Mr. J. L., how can I spread this salt and season the world?"

Mr. J. L. answered, "In a spiritual sense, salt is the word of God that we read out of the Bible. By you being a believer of God's word, you are the salt of the earth when you go forth and spread the word (salt). Salt, in a normal sense, will make you thirsty. Now, we spread the salt (God's word) for a more <u>noble and glorious purpose,</u> whereby it will serve as the fabric of holiness and make you thirsty for more of the Word. You will want water because, in a normal sense, salt will dry up water, and the water that it dries up represents your spiritual battle" (Ephesians <u>6:11-14).</u> "God's word (salt) will make you thirst for living water" (*<u>John 7:37-38; Psalm</u>*

42:1-2). "So, don't be a well or fountain without water," Mr. J.L. added (*2 Peter* 2:17). "Tell others about God's word. One must have substances (wisdom) to have water in their spiritual well" (*Hebrews* 11:1).

Thickpin asked, "So, when we believe in God's word (salt), we get a taste of the living water and want more?"

Mr. J. L. continued, "The Lord's word (salt) makes you thirsty, and at the same time, it will preserve you and make you thirsty for the living water. The Lord is a fountain of living water. Yes, when you get a taste of that living water, you will want to seek and get more" (*Jeremiah* 17:13).

"Now, here is one way you can get your thirst quenched. One, is if your grandparents, or a minister, have testified about what God has miraculously done for them" (*Exodus* 10:1-). "They keep the memory alive through testimonies for future generations. Hearing others testify makes you want more living water" (*Psalm* 42:1, 22). "Combined, the word and testimonies will quench your spiritual thirst and you can be full and want more, both to abound and suffer need" (*Philippians* 4:12).

Charlie asked, "How can I get more of this living water?"

"Here are several ways that you can get more of the living water," Mr. J.L. replied. "One would be when you sacrifice to God. When you have a choice to go out with your friends for some fun, but you choose to stay home and pray and read God's word instead. Another would be if you help someone in need. That is another example of a sacrifice. When you sacrifice to God, it's like putting money in the bank; this will give you more pleading power to plead to God" (*Acts* 7:3; *Philippians* 4:19). "When you do a good deed for someone else, it makes you feel good. This is a true sign: living water makes the inner man grow day by day as the outer man perishes" (2 *Corinthians* 4:16).

SALT II

On a Saturday morning some weeks later, after Mr. J.L. finished milking the cow and feeding the pigs and chickens, he got with the children again to continue their lesson about salt. They were drawn to Mr. J.L. like a magnet as he sat on the bench near the woodpile.

"How is everybody today?" he asked.

The children replied, "Good morning, Mr. J. L., and we are blessed."

Mr. J. L. said, "Today we will talk about how we can spread salt (God's word) of the earth" (*Matthew* 5:13). "How can you, as an individual, season the world through your activities?" (*Mark* 16:15).

Thickpin said, "We can share what we heard in church."

"Absolutely," Mr. J. L. replied. "When you spread God's word, you are doing two things: One, you're helping your fellow man to see with a spiritual insight. (*Mark* 16:15). Two, sacrificing your time for God's work (*Hebrews* 9:15). When you sacrifice for God or his people, He will pay you double for your trouble (*Job* 14:10). Everyone likes being paid double for their trouble. Yes?"

"Of course." Charlie replied.

Lewis asked, "But how do we do that?"

Mr. J. L. responded "When you sacrifice your time to spread God's word (salt) you may get closer to God by fasting and praying (*Mark* 9:27-29). This will equip you with more power to do God's will, let the oppressed go free, and break yokes. (*Isaiah* 58:6). Plus, Christians can plead for additional mercy for doing work for God (Acts 17:31). When you sacrifice, fast, and pray; try to get into the mind of the author of the word. God will supply all your needs according to his riches and glory by Jesus Christ" (Philippians 4:19). "Dedicate some time to God."

Thickpin said, "I began to feel the Spirit just by listing to you. Is that normal?"

Mr. J. L. replied, "Yes, that is perfectly normal because often a person will follow the **salt trail** you leave by the example, they see in you, and It will cause them to thirst for more of that living water" (Romans 2:15; John 7:37-38; Psalm 2:1-2).

Lewis asked, "How does this work?"

Mr. J. L. explained, "Process is the operative word. The life process goes as follows: Tribulation worketh patience, patience worketh experience, and experience worketh hope" (Romans 5:1-7). "Now, throughout life you will have opposition and opportunity. With God's help, do not let the opposition change your focus on your heart's desire" (Psalm 37:4). "**Blessings delayed are not blessings denied. God's word (salt) is living water and heaven and earth shall pass away before God's word fails**" (Matthew 24:35). "So, dig into God's word for pure living water. Always confess your sins to God and restore fellowship with Him" (John 1:9, Acts 3:19, 23). "When Moses and Aaron turned the Pharaoh's water to blood, the Egyptians were digging with gusto for water. So should you dig into the Bible for living water" (Exodus 7:2).

SALT III

Some weeks later, the children met with Mr. J. L. on Friday evening after school on their way home. Mr. J. L.'s mule was pulling a slide, and the kids loved to ride on it. Mr. J. L. stopped to let them get on. They played around to see who could stand while the slide was moving. When Mr. J. L. got back to his farm and had put the mule back in its stall, Mr. J. L. said a prayer for them and their families.

Mr. J. L. greeted the children, "Good evening. How are you all this evening?

"We are blessed," said the children together.

Mr. J. L. said, "So, do you remember that bacteria, fungi, and pathogens can't survive in a salt environment? According to God's word, in a similar way, salt eliminates ungodly activities, and they can't survive in a spiritual environment" (*Ephesians* 6:11-13).

"What happens if salt loses its savor?" Lewis asked.

Mr. J. L. responded, "If salt loses its savor, wherewith shall it be called salt? (Matt. 5:13). "You should return to God's word and replenish your heart and spirit in God's word because Satan will always return and seek whom he may devour" (*1 Peter* 5:8)

"It should start with your father and mother or some other spiritual-minded person's instruction" (*Proverbs* 1:8-9). "This is where your wisdom and understanding begin" (*Proverbs* 1:2; 2 Chronicles 7:1-11).

Charlie asked, "How can we maintain high salt?"

Mr. J. L. replied, "First, pay God daily—as many times as you wish" (1 Thessalonians 3:9). "Study God's word with meditation: try to get into the Author's mind" (2 Timothy 2:15). "When you look for God, you will find him because his temple is in you" (Jeremiah 29:12-13; *1 Corinthians* 3:16). "When you use God's word (salt), His word goes out and does what God intends; it does not return to Him void" (Isaiah 55:11; *Hebrews* 4:12).

Thickpin asked, "In what ways can we apply salt?"

Mr. J. L. answered him by saying, "Life Is full of choices and consequences" (*Proverbs* 6:6-11). "Here, opposition versus opportunity is revealed with the use of God's word. Remember, you are the salt of the earth" (*Matthew* 5:13). "Imagine you are a giant salt- shaker and you must season many. They will thirst for God's word."

Mr. J. L. continued, "At this point, you should begin to see the mystery of God's work (*Colossians* 2:26). "Again, imagine that you are a saltshaker. Your job is to sprinkle the salt (God's work) on all you meet, especially when you come from churches or when you read God's word and the Holy Spirit enlightens you on a particular passage. Now the thirst sets in on the person you shared the word with—your contact. Now is the time to ensure that their thirst is quenched with living water. By this time, they will have seen and experienced enough to trust in God's word. Trusting in God's word is like a tree planted by the water" (*Jeremiah* 17:7). "When a tree is planted by the water it will get plenty of nourishment from the water to grow. Now, at this point, Jesus is on the spiritual (mental) line for people during his work; tell him what you want" (*Ezekiel* 47:3, 8). "When you believe in Jesus, He is your water. You are planted with him and that where you get your spiritual nourishment to go in the spirit. This why Jesus died for all our sins and rose again. Now, as a tree planted by the water, we can call on him anytime and anywhere and he will answer. Wherever you are, you can call upon his Holy name."

SALT IV

A couple of weeks later, Mr. J. L. had another meeting with the kids on a Saturday morning. The children's parents could hardly wait to send them to Mr. J. L.'s place for their spiritual awakening.

"Good morning, Mr. J. L.," the children said together.

"Good morning," Mr. J. L. answered. "Now, starting where we left of the last time. Salt! God's word is the salt for the world.

"In a spiritual sense, as God-believing people, you are the salt of the earth" (*Matthew* 5:13). "And since you are God-believing people, when you seek God's word and use it, it has power. Remember, you preserve the savor of the salt by going back where you first met the Lord in his word, to include following the godliness you see in others" (*Romans* 2:15). Now, who can tell me what happens when you turn to God?" (*Zechariah* 1:3).

Lewis answered and said, "God loved us while we were still sinners" (*Romans* 5:8).

Mr. J.L. replied, "You can be full and still want more. God's word prepares us for more of God's spirit, and you get more" (*John* 3:34). "'I am knocking, and if you hear me, **COME!**'" (Revelation 3:20).

Mr. J. L. emphasized, "You can get more of the living water by digging into the Word (salt). The more of the preserving you get, the more thirst you will have for the living water" (*Jeremiah* 17:13). "Life is full of opportunities and opposition; opportunity presents itself to you and it might seem too good to be true. At that moment, your little faith in God's word is your opposition" (*Acts* 12:9; Galatians 6:10). "This especially means that when you have a chance to do something good for your fellow man, you should do it.

"One must have faith to overcome opposition" (*Hebrews* 11:1). "Sometimes, you have to go back and find who you left behind, 'O ye of little faith'" (*Luke* 2:45; *Matthew* 16:8).

"What other type of obstacles do we have to battle with?" Thickpin asked.

Mr. J. L. answered, this is a process. When you overcome hurdles of opposition and opportunity, then you must contend with choices and consequences, then anticipation and realization" (*Proverbs* 6:6; *2 Kings* 8:8–23). "Choices are when a chance to do something appears to you. Consequences are the backlash of the choices you have made. Anticipation and realization. Sometimes, anticipation is more exciting than realization."

Mr. J. L. then sang to them lyrics from an old, beloved Christian song.

> *When your back is against the wall,*
> *you feel like you like are going to fall,*
> *you are just right for a miracle in your life.*
> *You are just right for a miracle in your life,*
> *If you can't see it or feel it, expect it.*

When you thank and praise God for your blessings it is a marvelous thing. (1 Chronicle 30:23) "You have laid up in storage a good foundation against times to come" (*1 Timothy* 6:19). "No matter what situation you are in, God's word with the answer. Remember, Satan is always watching for you to make a misstep" (*1 Peter* 5:6–8; *Matthew*

10:16; *Ephesians* 6:13). "However, when you come on the scene or in the picture, God's word goes before you if you ask him" (*Proverbs* 3:6; Isaiah 55:11; *Hebrews* 4:12).

Charlie discovered for himself that God's word is multi-purposed for us. Charlie was talking to some youngsters who were threatening him, and he asked them a couple of biblical questions, such as, "Did you pay God today? Did you know that your mind is the table for your heart? What do you have on the table?" The other two young men stood frozen and stunned as they digested the parable. Charlie asked Mr. J.L., "Did I do the right thing?"

"Yes, Charlie. That is correct. It is the salt, the living water, and the light of the world you see. The Word reflects God upon us, and the smallest light can dispel darkness. Some love darkness rather than light because their deeds are evil. My grandmom used to sing, '**<u>This little light of mine, I'm gonna let it shine, let it shine, let it shine</u>**.'

"God's word is eternal" (*John* 8:12; *Matthew* 24:35). "Remember, God is always on the spiritual line between you and Him, so when we pray, He hears us because he never sleeps. God is in us" (*Psalm* 121:3). "If you need more courage to sprinkle salt on someone, just ask Him" (*Acts* 12:6). "The Lord is our God, our strength, and our song; He is our God, and He will prepare a habitation for us" (*Exodus* 15:2). Mr. J. L. added, "Remember, ye are the temple for God's Spirit" (*1 Corinthians* 6:19). "Confess your sins and restore your relationship with God" (*Psalm* 32:5). "When you request something from God, wait on Him" (*Psalm* 27:14). "It was three days before God raised Jesus from the dead or delivered Jonah from the whale's belly" (Luke 23:7-8; *Matthew* 12:4). "This is one way that God comes to our rescue." Most of all make sure that you are ready for the miracle or answer.

Grandpa Said

CHAPTER 2

GRANDPA SAID

Section 1

Grandpa's name was Lee, and he was a farmer. After the emancipation was signed, Lee was one of the lucky ones who received the forty acres and two miles from the government to farm. Lee and his family had been blessed by God in so many ways and he was very thankful for that. He could not read or write, but he had an extraordinarily strong memory. When he went to church and listened to the sermon, he would remember what the preacher said, chapter and verse. Then he would apply it to his experiences and invest it into the children through a spiritual prism. He would refer to his investment in the children as "woodpile talk." He would meet with the grandchildren and others on Friday evening or Saturday morning. There, he would answer their questions.

As Lee waited at the woodpile, the children came and said, "Good morning, Grandpa!" All the children called him Grandpa.

"Good morning, you all," Grandpa said. "We will talk about your days at school and some of the situations you are confronted with each day. So, what do you have to ask this morning?"

Sally was always energetic, so she asked Grandpa the first question, "Grandpa, what should I do when other school kids bully me?"

"Okay," said Grandpa." Little one, you must understand something about a bully. A bully is usually insecure in themselves. One, it is the work of the devil. Two, the devil is tempting you through your fellow man, through your weakness" (*1 John* 2:16, 4:4).

Charlie asked, "How does he know my weakness?" (This is the same Charlie from the previous chapter plus a couple of new children.)

"Well," said Grandpa, "temptation follows a pattern. There are three areas: one, lust of the flesh; two, lust of the eyes; and three, the pride of life, or self-interest" (*Job* 31:7). "They will bully you when you look scared" (*Jeremiah* 1:9). "God has your back" (*Isaiah* 52:12). "So, they are insecure with themselves and turn into a busybody" (*1 Timothy* 5:13).

Grandpa continued, "This is spiritual warfare, so we must put on the whole armor of God that ye may be able to stand against the wiles of the devil" (*Isaiah* 59:17) "We wrestle not against flesh and blood, but against principalities, against powers, the rulers of the darkness and spiritual wickedness" (*Ephesians* 6:11-13). "To fight this spiritual battle, allow God to direct your path, thank Him, then delight yourself in the Lord and He shall give you the desire of your heart" (*Proverbs* 3:6; *1 Chronicles* 23:30; *Psalm* 37:4).

Sally asked, "What about the bully?"

Grandpa replied, "Now, when your conscience is clear and you are as bold as a lion, be not afraid of their faces" (*Proverbs* 28:1; *Jeremiah* 1:8-9). "While the bully is still bullying, take them away mentally and spiritually into the Mountain, a spiritual place where they have never been before, and *ask* them, 'Did you pay God today?'" (*Revelation* 21:10; *1 Chronicles* 23:30). This means to elevate them in the spirit high above their normal mental and spiritual position.

Grandpa continued, "Ask them If they knew that their mind is the table for their heart" (*Proverbs* 3:3). "Make sure you don't have any dirty dishes on the table. This is salt. God's word" (Isaiah 55:11; *Hebrews* 4:12). "You are not alone" (*Heb.* 3:5).

Section 2

Several weeks later, the grandchildren returned for more wisdom. This time, the children were there before Grandpa because he was still slopping the pigs.

"Hello, Grandpa! We are here."

"Okay," said Grandpa Lee. "I'll be there in a minute."

"Good morning. How are you all this morning?"

Sally, Jojo, and Charlie all said, "Good morning, Grandpa."

"Okay," Grandpa said, "the last time we talked about the bullies at school."

Charlie said, "There are so many bullies at school."

Jojo asked, "How do we prepare for such engagements?"

Grandpa replied, "The bullies are used as tools by the devil to terrorize people. The bully preys on what they perceive to be a soft target—your weakness" (1 *John* 2:16). "When you sprinkle the word of God on him, it disrupts this tactic.

"Remember the little ants and how they work together and prepare for the future?" (*Proverbs* 6:6). "Have compassion in your heart for the bully while you sprinkle the word of God on him" (*Luke* 15:20). "Your planning should include being ministered to God by thanking Him and knowing who

He is. He is omnipotent, meaning He has all power. He is omnipresent, which means that He is everywhere at the same time. And, He is omniscient, meaning God has all knowledge" (*Matthew* 19:26; *Psalm* 44:21, 139:7-10). So, learn the Ten Commandments and *Psalm* 23. "At home, your parents will teach you the basics of spiritual of life, like the Lord's Prayer. Make sure you understand them well (*Matthew* 6:9; Psalm 23). As you grow, God will send you forth as sheep in the midst of wolves, who are the bullies. So, be wise as a serpent and harmless as a dove" (*Matthew* 10:16). "God will protect you, all you have to do is use His word."

Sally asked, "What can poor sheep do with wolves?"

Grandpa continued, "When you pray, thank God and He will give you power to tread on serpents and scorpions, and nothing shall by any means hurt you" (*Luke* 10:18-19).

"That's powerful, Grandpa." Patsy said.

Grandpa replied, "Now take them away in the spirit with a series of questions, taking the fight to the devil" (*Revelation* 17:3; *Ephesians* 6:14-17). "Now, start feeding them the word of God. Be not afraid of their faces" (*Jeremiah* 15:3-7). "Ask the bully in a soft voice, 'What is the table for the heart?' The answer is the mind" (*Proverbs* 15:1). "Make sure you don't have any dirty dishes on it" (*Proverbs* 3:3). "Is a well without water still a well? "The answer is no, because it has no substance" (*2 Peter* 2:17). What are the two most important dates in your life? The answer is: The day you were born and why you were born" (*Job* 14:13-14). "Remember, God never sleeps" (*Psalm* 121:3). "God has your back" (*Isaiah* 52:12). "You see, when you say something like that, it will make the bully soul-search in God's word. This will set them back and make them think, and they will forget about bullying."

Section 3

Some days later, they visited Grandpa again, and naturally their grandpa was ready as always to answer their questions.

JoJo asked, "How do I get rid of the temptations of Satan?"

Grandpa replied, "Satan will only go away for a season" (*Luke* 4:13). "Then he will be back on the job again. Satan tempted Jesus, and Jesus defied Satan's temptation by relying on the Author of the scripture of God" (*1 John* 2:16). "The Author of the Scripture is God. His word is quick and powerful, and sharper than a two-edged sword" (*Hebrews* 4:12). "Christ is your preventive medicine against Satan" (*Hebrews* 7:25). "You will never get rid of him; but with God, you can cast him out for a season" (*Matthew* 8:16; *Luke* 4:13). "You will never get rid of temptation, but you can keep it at bay by praying to keep it at bay."

Jojo asked, "How do we keep Satan at bay? Will he always be there?"

Grandpa answered, Yes! But "The Lord is omnipresent, everywhere at the same time, and He is our Shepherd" (*Matthew* 6:9). "That means, He will go before us if we ask him" (*Proverbs* 3–6). "And when He goes before us, He goes before us with all His omnipotent power and all His omniscient knowledge. When you meet a bully, ask him if he paid God today" (*1 Chronicles* 23:30). "Ask the bully, 'Who are you?' Then let him know who you are—God's word (salt). 'By the grace of God, I am what I am'" (*1 Corinthians* 15:10). "The **Grace** of God is with me. Learn His word and use his word out of the Bible: words, characters, letters, and phrases" (*Matthew* 8:16).

"Now, Children," Grandpa continued as he handed them each a piece of paper and a pencil, "I want you to write down the following passages of scripture: Matthew 8:16, John 3:34,

Luke 10:18-19, Jeremiah 5:14 and 23:29, and James 3:6-8. When you get home, I want you to read them."

Section 4

Some days later on a Friday evening, Grandpa entertained the grandchildren again with words of wisdom and understanding. This time, he was waiting for them at the woodpile.

Grandpa said, "Good evening to you all."

"Good evening to you, Grandpa!" said all the children together.

Grandpa said, "Okay, we will talk about the signs of the times and God answering your prayers. The signs of the times will take its toll on the bully. When you have God on your side, He will make you strong enough to withstand anything that the bullies can dish out. Just God's word will dismantle the bully's operation" (Hebrews 4:12; Isaiah 55:11). "Then it's just a matter of time before the bully comes after you one way and God will make them flee seven ways" (Deuteronomy 28:7).

"What are some of these signs?" Charlie asked.

Grandpa said, "Okay, think about it. One blood of humanity can be used in all nations the world over" (*Acts* 17:26). "It's clear to me that we are all brothers and sisters of the same blood in a spiritual sense if we all love God and do his will" (*Matthew* 12:50). "We look different by virtue of what environment our ancestors developed out of. All believers who believe in God praise God."

Jojo asked, "So, does this mean that God will answer their prayers, too?"

Grandpa replied, "God is in every man. You just have to find Him" (2 *Corinthians* 6:1). "When you find God, serve him with joy and gladness" (Deuteronomy 28:47) "God will bless you according to his riches" (*Ephesians* 3:16). "Additionally, believer may plead for God's mercy" (*Acts* 17:31).

"Now, believers should remain in an attitude of prayer" (*1 Thessalonians* 5:16-17). "'Pray without ceasing'" (*1 Thessalonians* 5:17). "'Watch and pray'" (*Mark* 13:33). "Lay up prayer in storage for yourself against times to come. Building up the good things you do is one way to lay up prayers in storage" (*1 Timothy* 6:19).

Jojo asked, "How can I do this?"

Grandpa reminded them, "Don't forget God" (*Luke* 2:14-52). "When things are going well, still pay God in the currency of thanksgiving" (*1 Thessalonians.* 3:9; *1 Chronicles* 23:30). "This will strengthen your faith" (*Matthew* 27:63). "Your request can be fulfilled in an instant or up to three days, depending on your faith. For example, in *Mark* 5:25-30, 40, Jesus heals at a distance" (*John* 4:47-52; *Matthew* 15:32-39). "All of these are signs of the times. As you get older, you will see more and understand more.

"Remember, never lie. Sometimes, you cannot go forward because you forgot where you came from. Never forget your origins, and if you change your thinking, you change your life."

Grandpa continued, "Learn all you can about everything you can. Your brain is a muscle; the more you use it, the greater your learning capacity will become. And remember, an empty wagon makes a lot of noise. Amen!"

Grandma Said

CHAPTER 3

GRANDMA SAID

Section 1

Grandma's name was Rose, and she was the one who held everything together. She was the finance minister for the family. She had a wide range of talents: reading, writing, cooking, sewing, and disciplining the young ones to develop their character. Grandpa did all the physical work, from sun-up till sundown. (The grandkids only lived about two-hundred yards down the road.) Grandpa was a strong man and creative, with everything he touched. The grandchildren's mother died when the youngest child was just six months old. Now the boy was eight and the girl had just turned ten years old.

Grandma told us to bathe in a foot tub and taught us how to wash, make starch, and iron our clothes. Her main interest in us was to make sure that we knew God. Grandma taught us to have an attitude of gratitude, so we would gather around the porch when she is rocking in her rocking chair while knitting. It seemed that she enjoyed us asking her questions. We all spoke together when we would gather there.

"Good morning, Grandma!"

"Good morning, Samuel, Rachel, and Sarah, my blessed grands. What questions do you have for me this morning?"

"Grandma, what must I do to grow up and be wise like you?" Samuel asked.

"Well, let me see," Grandma began. "Let's start with the basics: Believe that Jesus was crucified, that He was dead and buried, and that on the third day, God raised him from the dead and he ascended into heaven, that whosoever believes on him will have life after death, life everlasting" (*Romans* 10:9). "Believe in God almighty, serve Him, and pay Him a minimum of twice a day" (*Genesis* 17:1; *1 Chronicles* 23:30; *Ephesians* 5:20). "Then, acknowledge him in all thy ways and He will direct your path" (Proverbs 3:6). "Now, if you have invited God in your life, He will always be wherever you are" (1 Corinthians 9:19-25). "My grandson, accept these words of wisdom, be quick to listen, slow to speak, and slow to anger" (*Proverbs* 29:20; 16:32). "Remember, a fool is counted as wise when he shuts his lips" (*Proverbs* 17:28).

Samuel replied, "Okay, Grandma. I will try to do this the next time I'm being provoked" (*Proverbs* 16:32, 1:8).

Rachel asked, "Grandma, how do I move toward my vision and my dream?" (*Joel* 2:28).

"Granddaughter Rachael, God gives grace to the humble" (Proverbs1:8-9). "Let your life be set in the eyes of the Lord" (*1 Samuel* 26:24). "Resist the proud but give grace to the humble" (*James* 4:6) "So, humble yourselves so that you may go far with the Lord. Even when you pass through water, he will be with thee, rivers shall not overflow on you, and you will walk through fire and not get burned" (*Isaiah* 43:2). "When you keep your dream as a vision, you will always have energy to make your vision become a reality."

Rachael replied, "Grandma, you have helped me see the light of truth. I had become prideful because I was honored above everyone in the class with my good grades. I guess I'd better bring myself down a notch" (*Ephesians* 4:32).

Grandma said, "My dear child, compare not yourself among yourselves for this is not wise" (*2 Corinthians* 10:12–14). "And for goodness' sake, don't stretch yourself beyond your measure" (*2 Corinthians* 10:13–15).

Rachael said, "So, Grandma. If I just be myself and be humble to God and believe by confessing with my mouth that Jesus was crucified dead and buried, and believe in my heart that God raised Jesus from the dead, and that whosoever believes shall be saved then say my prayers, will I be alright, Grandma?" (*Matthew* 6:9).

"Absolutely!" Grandma said, "And pay God with thanks a minimum of twice daily" (*2 Chronicles* 23:30; *Ephesians* 5:20; *1 Thessalonians*. 3:9; *Daniel* 6:10).

Section 2

Some days later, on Saturday morning, the children gathered around their Grandma again and greeted her.

"Hello, Grandma," they said together.

"Hello, Samuel, Rachael, and Sarah!"

"So, you all want to know what to do to be blessed like me. Well," said Grandma, "start by feeding your soul by finding Jesus and believing in God" (*Matthew* 22:37; *Mark* 12:30; *Luke* 10:27). "Then, be saved" (*Romans* 10:9). "Then, make it a part of your daily life to thank God a minimum of two times a day" (*1 Chronicles* 23:30, *Ephesians* 5:20). "Now God will be wherever you are because you found God within you, the temple of the Holy Ghost" (*1 Chronicles* 9:19–25, *1 Corinthians* 6:19).

"All these passages of scripture speak of how one may connect with our Lord."

"Dad said that we have two important dates in our lives," said Samuel (*Job* 14:13-14).

"Samuel, that is so true," Grandma said. "Everyone has a proper gift from God" (*1 Corinthians* 7:7). "Some have a coat of many colors" (*Genesis* 37:3-32). "Joseph had many gifts and talents. Everything has a process that it goes through" (*Proverbs* 24:3-5). "After you go through a process, it can't be reversed."

Rachael asked, "Grandma, you mean like the plants when they grow?"

"Exactly!" said Grandma. "So, when plants grow, they encounter weeds and so on" (*Matthew* 13:27-40). "Now, when man grows, he also faces challenges, both physical and spiritual. So, this means there are always oppositions and opportunities" (*Acts* 12:12-15).

Sarah asked, "What do we do then, Grandma?"

Grandma continued, "When you feel weak and have doubt, pray for God to strengthen you" (*Proverbs* 25:28). "Say your prayers" (*Matthew* 6:9). "Remember when you say, 'Thy kingdom come' in the Lord's Prayer. That closes out all evil spirits. You will always be tempted when you do good things" (*1 John* 2:16). "Remember, Satan comes in many different forms, so be ready for battle" (1 Peter 5:8). "Be ready" (*Isaiah* 59:17). "To really get serious with your devotion to God, sacrifice by missing a meal or don't do something that you really like to do and pray to God instead" (*Hebrews* 9:15) "This sacrifice is like putting money in the bank" (*1 Timothy* 6:19). "Always thank God and study His word, remembering the book, chapter, and verse" (*Ephesians* 5:20). "As an example, consider *Psalm* 64:3. Keep your conscience clear"

(1 *John* 1:9) "Do not let the sun set with wrath on your mind" (*Ephesians* 4:26-27). "Do not compare yourself with others" (*2 Corinthians*. 10:12-14) "Be mindful of your tongue" (*James* 3:6-8). **Amen!**

Section 3

The grandkids met with Grandma again on a Saturday evening after they had finished all their chores. Some of the grandkids' chores was feeding and watering the chickens.

"Good evening, Grandma!" said Samuel said. Sarah and Rachael were a little grumpy this evening because they wanted to stay home and play jacks, but Samuel told them to come along and learn something.

"My, my, you all look good, healthy, clean, and you're so well-mannered," said Grandma. "Do you have some questions for Granny today?" Sarah and Rachael, you all look a little sad. Okay, I will hopefully give you some information that will cheer you up and make it worth your time to be here."

Samuel asked, "What are you knitting, Grandma?"

"I am knitting a sweater for the cold weather days that are coming this winter," Grandma replied (*Proverbs* 6:6-11). "I fear the cold winter, which is God's work. I fear God, which is the beginning of wisdom, and knowledge of holiness is understanding. Understanding is to know what is true and false, good, and bad, what matters and what does not. So, as you grow into young men and women, you should focus on building your house with wisdom and understanding" (*Proverb*s 9:10).

Samuel asked, "What will happen if we build our life without it?"

Grandma continued, "It is possible your life could be like a shipwreck" (*1 Timothy* 1:19). "With wisdom and understanding you will be a prudent person" (*Proverbs* 27:12). "With those two factors you won't miss out on what life is all about" (*Proverbs* 9:1-18). "You will know what life is about because your father and mother will have properly taught you. It is time for the son become prudent enough in his decisions as to whom to follow" (*Proverbs* 9:1). "You see, no one is perfect, but it's the tribulations we endure and the people we meet along the way that make us who we are. Remember, God has empowered angels to appear in human form to His servants" (*Hebrews* 13:2). "Always ask for guidance" (*Proverbs* 3:6). "If you want a sign to confirm something, He will give you a sign" (*2 Samuel* 5:17-25).

Sarah asked, "Do you get all this help when you believe in God?"

Grandma said, "Yes, my little one. God can do much more than I can say. A wise person will get advice from many people of good judgement before making decisions" (*Proverbs* 11:14).

Rachael said, "Grandma, I have a gift."

"What gift do you have, Rachael?" Grandma asked.

"I love to sing," Rachael replied. "Especially spiritual songs."

Grandma said, "You have a gift? Good! Work on it and improve it" (*Proverbs* 19:16). "Be a self-starter like the ant" (*Proverbs* 6:6). "Do something with what you have, and you'll be given more" (*John* 3:34). "Do not use what you have unwisely, or it could be taken away" (*Mark* 4:25). "Remember, God's word is a light to your path and a lamp unto your feet" (*Psalm* 119:105). "In this situation, God will guide you with spirit to where you are supposed to go.

Grandma Said

Grandma continued, "Learn all you can about everything you can. Good things. Remember, an empty wagon makes lots of noise. Don't be an empty wagon."

Build on Your Vision

CHAPTER 4

Build on Your Vision

Section 1

Mr. King drove a tractor on a large plantation for one of the wealthy farmers in the area. He would always encourage children to follow their dreams and their vision. He would tell the children to use what they already have to get what they want in the future. In this little part of the country everyone was interested in investing in the children.

Some of the kids said, "The only thing I have is this hoe in my hand, so I can weed the cotton and corn."

Mr. King said, "You have more than that. You have a sound mind, you have your brain, you have your will to do better, and you surely believe in yourself. So, now we are going to make sure that you have God at the helm of your activities."

From time to time, Mr. King, who was also a Sunday School teacher, would go by the playground at the church and have a little chat with the children. There were no air conditioners in this little holy church, so the class that included **Main**, **M.C**., **Lonnie**, and **Thickpin**, was held outside under the big oak tree in the church yard.

"Good Morning, Mr. King!" said some of the children.

"Good morning, you all!" Mr. King said, returning the greetings. "Today, we will talk about building on your vision."

Mr. King asked, "Have you ever laid on the ground, looked skyward, and just let your mind wonder or daydream?"

Lonnie said, "Yes. I begin to see things that no one else can see but me. What's supposed to happen then?"

Mr. King said, "While you are lying or sitting there, your daydream turns into imagination that produces a clear vision" (*Joel* 2:28).

"A vision about what?" Main asked.

"Well," said Mr. King, "a vision about being a doctor, a rancher, playing music, a farmer, writing and singing songs, and so on. Imagination is a tool your heart uses to get what it wants. God is in you and He fuels your imagination" (*1 Corinthians* 7:9). "It does so by producing a vision that is motivating enough for you to act upon. Vision allows you to act coherently with focus and determination over long spans of time" (*Romans* 1:17). "Remember, the temple of God is in you" (*1 Corinthians* 7:19). "He is in your heart where your imagination originates" (*1 Corinthians* 3:16). "Focus on the things in your vision that interest you" (*1 Corinthians* 7:7). "Move quickly and start preparing for your miracle, gathering the resources you will need to support your miracle preparation and readiness" (*Philippians* 3:14; *2 Kings* 3:10–20). "Dig some ditches" (*John* 9:6–12). "Remember the story about the five loaves and two fish. Five-thousand men had to prepare for the miracle by sitting down in groups of fifties and hundreds to get ready for the miracle. God normally won't give you a miracle unless you are ready for one" (2 Kings 3:10).

"Don't forget to pay God" (*1 Thessalonians* 3:9). "A body without spirit is dead" (*James* 3:26). "When you prepare for more spiritual power, you will get more without measure" (*John* 3:34). "So, get a move on with your vision. Get to work; don't just sit there and let your vision become a bygone dream" (*2 Kings* 7:1-6). "Give God something to work with. He will always help you."

M.C. asked, "Mr. King, can you give us an example, Sir?"

"Okay", Mr. King said. "Jesus fed five-thousand men, plus women and children, with five loaves and two fish. Jesus made the people ready for the miracle. He had them sit down on the green grass in groups of fifties and hundreds. So, you see, Jesus prepared them for the miracle that was to be. So, to be a good player on a football team, you must sacrifice some time to practice instead of doing something else that will not enhance your football skills. The quarterback will not throw the football where you are, he will throw the football where you are supposed to be. If you are there to catch the ball, then that is your small miracle. So, to get your blessing, you must move quickly and get into position to receive your blessing" (*Philippians* 3:14).

Mr. King continued, "Remember, don't go around telling everybody your vision or dream" (*Isaiah* 59:1-9; *Genesis* 37:1-17). "Move quickly on your vision like Peter did" (Acts 12:6-9). "Now, your vision is the opportunity knocking. Let it in and move to the next level of blessing" (*Acts* 12:13-16). "Life is full of opportunities and oppositions. So, don't be your own opposition because you didn't move and take advantage of the opportunity."

Lonnie said, "That's clear to me now. Even the blind can see that mentally and spiritually."

Section 2

Two weeks later, due to the Sunday rotation within the church, Mr. King is their Sunday school teacher again. This time, Mr. King decided to have a review, just to check his pupils' retention.

"Good morning, you all!" Mr. King said.

"Good morning, Mr. King," they said together.

"Okay," said Mr. King, "Let us review what we discussed about the process of a vision. A process is a series of actions that is taken to achieve a particular end. A process cannot be reversed."

Mr. King asked for a volunteer go give a quick review.

Lonnie raised his hand and stood, "Imagination comes out of the heart where God has placed your gifts and talents. You let your mind begin to wonder, then your imagination produces a vision that motivates you to act upon it. Vision makes you focus on what you see in your imagination."

M.C. added, "The vision allows you to act coherently with focus."

"Very good," Mr. King said. "I'm proud of both of you. Vision, with focus and determination over a long span of time. Now we will discuss some other arrows that you need in your quiver as you grow in Christ on this spiritual adventure" (*Isaiah* 22:6; *Romans* 4:20). Since we are on a spiritual adventure, you will need some tools and weapons" (Romans 4:20). "God's word is sharper than a two-edged sword; it's like a hammer" (*Hebrews* 4:12; *Jeremiah* 23:29). "Also among your weapons are The Lord's Prayer and your parents' instruction" (*Matthew* 6:9; *Psalm* 23; *Proverbs*1:8–9). "What more do we need?" Mr. King asked.

"There will always be problems, so you will need to know a problem-solving process. Step one is to recognize the problem. Step two is to make an estimate of the situation. step three, determine the cause. For step four, list some possible solutions. And step five is to take action. Now, pay God for your wondering" (*Ephesians* 5:20). "Develop a passion with the many gifts you were born with. Then, put your little in God's hand and He will make it much" (*Luke* 9:13).

Lonnie asked, "How do I get passion, and will I know when it comes?"

Mr. King said, "You will know that your passion for your gift has increased because sometimes you'll rather do it than eat, for example. In other words, you will be full of desire and still want more because you will be hungry for the development of your gift" (Philippians 4:12).

"Okay," Mr. King explained, "you may also evaluate your passion for your gift by fasting and praying" (*Mark* 9:29). "On this spiritual adventure you will be tempted many times" (Romans 4:20). "Just remember to put on the whole armor of God" (*Isaiah* 59:17). "Take the fight to the devil" (*Ephesians* 6:14-17). "Then, go forth using God's word and praying to God" (*Isaiah* 55:11).

Section 3

Some weeks later, the children came to Mr. King's house. Mr. King was a little exhausted, but he had a passion for investing in the neighborhood children. So, he spent some time with them.

"Good evening, Mr. King!" said the children.

"Good evening Charlie, Lewis, and Thickpin!" Mr. King said. "I pray that all is well with your families. All praise and thanks to God" (*Ephesians* 5:20). "We will discuss any point that is not clear to you."

Thickpin asked, "How do we prepare for life's journey?

"Well, "said Mr. King, "you start out listening to your parents and learning the golden rule: Do unto others as you want them to do unto you. Your parents' instruction should be an ornament on your head and a chain about your neck" (Proverbs 1:8–9). "Then you are faced with temptation" (*1 John* 2:16). "Be filled with wisdom and understanding" (Proverbs 9:10). "Praise and thank God" (*1 Chronicles* 23:30). "Fill your mind and heart with God's word, which is the most powerful word in the universe" (*Isaiah.* 55:11; *Hebrew*s 4:12). "When you believe in God, you have additional pleading power for His mercy" (*Acts* 17:31). "Remember to thank God. When you pray at the end of the day, include this scripture in your prayers: 'Keep me while I sleep, speak to me when you wake me, and direct me as I go'" (*Proverbs* 6:22).

Charlie said, "Yes, I've learned that before."

Mr. King said, "Yes, you did. Now I'll give you additional information that will benefit you in more than one way" (*Hebrews* 4:12). "Now for the two-edged sword. With this you can expand your mind. In Sunday School, we exercise and expand your memory capacity by memorizing God's word, thereby equipping you with spiritual ammunition to fight evil men" (*Ephesians* 6:11–13). "Now, your weapon is the word of God" (*Isaiah 55:12*; *Hebrews 4:12*). "Here are some examples: Someone walks up to you and says you told them a lie when you did not. Reply with *Matthew* 7:4. If someone insults you, give them a dose of *Psalm 64:3*. When someone talks about you to others, spreading rumors, that is a busybody. Give them 1 Timothy 5:13. A busybody is like a useless vine running all over the place, without a purpose or direction"

(*Ezekiel* 15:3-7). "If someone tries to shame you, ask them, 'Is a well without water still a well?' No water means no life or fertility. They need to either get a life or be a well without water. Tell them *2 Peter* 2:17."

Lewis said, "That will hit them like a ton of bricks."

"Keep in mind that the mind is the table for the heart and there could be some dirty dishes on the table. Tell them *Proverbs* 3:3. If one's eyes follow some sort of distraction, like a girl or guy, let them know it is better to follow the heart and not the eyes by telling them *Job 31:7*.

"Remember, God's word is like a fire, and like a hammer that breaketh rocks in pieces" (*Jeremiah* 23:39) Jesus' word and your faith can cast out devils" (*Matthew* 8:16). "Be mindful of your tongue" (*James* 3:6-8). "Remember, you are sheep in the midst of wolves, but the Lord gave you enough in your arsenal to handle all situations" (*Matthew 10:16*; *Luke* 10:18-19; *Psalm* 92:9-15). "Evil against evil destroys itself" (*Luke* 11:17).

"Now you are better equipped to overcome opposition and seize your opportunity to move forward with your vision" (*Acts* 12:13-16). "Don't get in your own way. Be bold in your faith" (*Proverbs* 28:1). "Remember, God's word is a lamp unto your feet, and a light to your path" (*Psalm* 119:105). And always protect your heart" (*Proverbs* 4:20).

Bully Medicine and Focus

CHAPTER 5

Bully medicine and focus

Section 1

Mr. John was full of wisdom and understanding as well as a beloved Sunday School teacher and deacon at Christian Light Missionary Baptist Church. In the summertime, when he conducted Bible study, Mr. John always had time to invest in the children. Sometimes, he would be asked a question when he was at the country store and He would take time to answer the child's question. Mr. John normally would conduct Bible study on Wednesday evening. The children loved to come because he always had a real-life story to go along with his teaching.

"Good evening, Mr. John," said the children.

"Good evening, Elijah, Paul, and Sally!" They were always the first three children.

Mr. John said, "Let us talk about bullies today."

Sally asked, "Why do we have bullies in school, anyway?"

"Well," Mr. John said, "humans operate with spirits from within themselves. Long ago, in the Garden of Eden, Eve was beguiled (bullied) by the serpent (snake) to eat from the

Tree of Knowledge of Good and Evil" (*Genesis* 2;17). So, Eve ate and gave some to her husband" (Genesis 3:6). "They both disobeyed God. They were cursed, but God still gave them clothing to protect them from the elements" (*Genesis* 3:14-21). "The world was made with God's word, and when we believe in God and use His word it is just as powerful now as it was in the beginning of time. Know who you are fighting" (*Ephesians* 6:11-13).

Elijah asked, "How can we fight him when we can't see him?"

Mr. John cleared his throat and said, "So, you must prepare for this battle, as *Isaiah 59:17* states. Remember, this is spiritual warfare, and to advance you must use the spirit of God's word to advance on the evil one. Now that you know who you are fighting, you can take the fight to Satan" (*Ephesians* 6:14-17). "Be not afraid of the bullies' faces" (Jeremiah 15:3-7). "Now take the fight to the devil" (Ephesians 6:14-17). "Your main weapon is God's word" (Hebrews 4:12; *Isaiah* 55:11). "Remember, bullies attack you because of their own weaknesses. Make it a point to memorize some Bible verses like *Matthew* 7:4, 1 *Timothy* 5:13, *Proverbs* 26:18-20, *Psalm* 64:3, and *Proverbs* 16:24, for starters. Ask the bully if he paid God today" (*1 Chronicles* 23:30). "Mind you, this is a lifelong battle because when you fight the evil devil off one time, he will only leave for a season" (*Luke* 4:13). "He will come back again and again. You must pray and watch" (*1 Peter* 5:6-8). "You can use any one or two of the scriptures and it that will get the job done."

"Remember, God is greater than he that is in the world" (*1 John* 4:4). "Make sure you are right when you take on the evil spirit in someone because God don't bless no mess" (*James* 4:3). "Learn a church song or a spiritual song or moan the song in a low voice and the devil in someone will want know what you are talking about. God will know, and He will take that joyful noise, bless it, and it will accomplish what God's servant needs" (*Isaiah* 55:11). "Always acknowledge God in all that you do, and He will direct you" (Proverbs 3:6). "Have a special place to pray. Knock, and the door will be opened; ask, and it shall be given to you" (*Matt.* 7:7-8). "You can hum or moan a prayer and God will know what you are talking about. True believers get more mercy" (*Acts* 17:31).

"Now, I'm beginning to see." Paul said.

Mr. John added, "Yes. God's word will bring you out of the darkness that your bully creates on you. The Lord is my light and salvation; whom shall I fear?" (*Psalm* 27:1). "God will not suffer you to be tempted above what you are able to handle" (1 Corinthians 10:13). "When the bully comes, you ask them, 'How can one be full and still be hungry?'" (*Philippians.* 4:19; *Hebrews*11:1). "Let them know that they whet their tongue like a sword and bend their bow and shoot bitter words" (*Psalm* 64:3). "Tell them to look in the mirror and ask that person, 'Who are you?'"

Section 2

Paul said to Mr. John, "You have been around for some years being blessed by the Almighty. How did you make it?"

"Well," said Mr. John began, "I made it by trusting in the almighty God" (Genesis 17:1). "You see, for me, this journey started a long time ago, but on this journey, we are not like material things. The older an item of material is, the less it's worth, but the older a child of God is, the more they are worth" (*Matthew* 10:28-31; 2 Corinthians 4:16).

Paul asked, "How do you deal with various temptations?"

Mr. John responded, "First, find out how to fight temptation. It is spirit. To wage spiritual warfare, you must believe in the One who has all power, all knowledge, and is always present. On this journey, you will be tempted. However, you will be tempted according to your weakness" (*1 John* 2:16). "And on this journey, you will have many battles with the spirit. Now, man has both a good and evil nature: the flesh against the spirit and the spirit against the flesh" (*Galatians* 5:17–27). On this journey, you have different winds in life, like a ship that sails on the water.

One ship drives east and another drives west with the same wind that blows. It is the way you set your sail and not the gale that gives your ship the direction to go.

Like the wind of fate as we voyage along through life, it is the set of the heart that decides its goal and not the calm or the strife.

Sally asked, "Why can't somebody just tell you what to do?"

Mr. John answered, "Most of the time, I hear a very light voice that I follow, but you must know your own signs with God" (*2 Samuel* 5:17–24). "It says in Hebrews 13:2, 'Entertain someone when your spirit guides you. Thereby, some entertain angles unaware.' Be sober, and be vigilant, because the devil seeks whom he may devour" (*1 Peter* 5:6–8). "In order to fight temptation, you must know yourself and always seek self-improvement. Have faith in God and in yourself (*Hebrews* 11:1).

"When you ask for God's guidance, He will even show you or tell you the answer in a dream" (*Proverbs* 3:6; *Genesis* 40:5, 41:15). "During your travels in life, don't forget that God made man a helpmate so that man would not be alone" (Genesis 2:18). "Even just to have a woman as a friend is great.

Remember, she was created as your helper and she does that very well" (*Joshua* 6:3-25).

Section 3

The children met with Mr. J. L. at Sunday School and the children were full of questions because they had thought about the information that they had received at the last Sunday School meeting with Mr. John.

After the children and Mr. John exchanged morning greetings, Mr. John said, "Today, we will discuss solving problems with God's help. So, I will ask some questions to get you started. This class will just be questions and answers."

Mr. John began, "What is the process you will use to solve the many problems you will face in life?"

Elijah responded to the question. The problem-solving process consist of five stages. 1. Recognize the problem, 2. Make an estimate of the situation, 3. Determine the cause, 4. Make a list of possible solutions, 5. Take action to solve the problem.

"Well, you are correct, Elijah," said Mr. John. "Now, let me see. Solving problems requires a process. First, believe in God. He is omnipotent; He has unlimited power. He is omniscient; He has unlimited knowledge, and He is omnipresent—always present, everywhere at the same time" (*Revelation* 19:6). "There is no one more qualified to have your back" (*Isaiah* 52:12).

Mr. John asked, "How does this process work, and what does all this mean?

Lewis said, "Okay, start with yourself by looking in the mirror and remember, when you point your index finger at someone, you have three fingers pointing back at you. Now, you may look elsewhere, since you are not the problem: One, now you have recognized the problem. Two, make an estimate of the situation. In other words, is the problem too massive for you to handle alone, or will you need help? Three, determine the cause. What led up to this situation? Exercise your deductive and inductive reasoning skills to evaluate the process. Four, pray and make a list of possible solutions. Do not compare yourself to others" (*2 Corinthians* 10:12-14). "Ask the Lord to direct you" (*Proverbs* 3:6). "Five, take action."

Elijah asked, "What experience do you have to share with us, Mr. John?"

Mr. John said, "Well, yes...Some clarifications for an instant review. I do have some experience in that arena, and at the end of the process, a decision will have to be made. First, begin with prayer" (*1 Thessalonians* 5:6-18). "Second, define the issue. Take counsel from God's people: pastors, lawyers, and believing friends, that you may be wise in the end" (*Proverbs* 5:20). "Third, seek biblical wisdom, which is a lamp to your feet and a light to your path" (*Proverbs* 119:105). "Fourth, seek God's counsel. Without it, you probably will be disappointed" (*Proverbs* 15:22). "Fifth, *trust God* with the decision" (*Proverbs* 3:5-8). "Sixth, be willing to admit mistakes and adjust accordingly. God will correct thee in measure, and not leave thee" (*Jeremiah* 46:28). "God will not put more on you than you can bear" (*1 Corinthians* 10:13). "Seventh, give praise to God for your success. Boast in His name forever" (*Psalm* 44:8). "Never forget to pay God. Thank him morning and evening" (*1 Chronicles* 23:30).

"When you ask God for help on a decision, you need to be sober and vigilant because your adversary is walking about seeking whom he may devour" (*1 Peter* 5:8). "Now you can do some angelic duties. God will work through you. So, give someone a pleasant word" (*Proverbs* 16:24). "Believers get more power to plead to God" (*Acts* 17:31).

Section 4

The previous session was questions and answers, and the children could barely wait for the next session. The students rushed over for the next evening and greeted Mr. John, who returned the greeting.

Mr. John asked, "Who are we, and why were we born?"

"Well," Paul replied, "it all started in the Garden of Eden, when the serpent beguiled Eve to eat fruit from the apple tree and gave some to her mate and they did eat, and they sinned" (*Genesis* 3:1-13). "Then God cursed the serpent, and he shall crawl on his belly all his days" (*Genesis* 3:14). "It has been said that the lump on the front of your throat is the Adam's apple. That's the core from the apple that Adam ate." Paul also added, "We are created a little lower than an angel" (*Psalm* 8:5).

Mr. John added, "You are not to forget that you were born with a talent, and with that talent you will contribute toward fulfilling your purpose in this world. In conversation, soft words and a soft voice destroy anger" (*Proverbs* 15:1).

Sally said, "So, this matches what you told us before about the temptation process" (*1 John* 2:6).

"Yes," Mr. John said, "but God gave you all the options. He gave you choices and consequences. A snack was taken from the Tree of Life, so man is born into sin, knowing good and evil" (*Genesis* 2:17). "To help us, God sent His son to die to pay for our sins" (*1 Thessalonians* 4:14). "Then, God gave us His words in the Bible" (*Isa.* 55:11). "So, when you are tempted by someone with an evil spirit, put God's word on them. Ask them, is a well without water still a well?" (*2 Peter* 2:17). "The answer for you is that your well will always have cool running water because you are in God's company and your substance is faith; that's your water (*Hebrews* 11:1, 4:12).

"Remember, God created the universe with just His word" (*Genesis* 1:1-4; *Isaiah* 55:11). "So, you can use any quote out of the Bible to fight Satan and his evil. He will leave you for a season, then return" (*James* 4:7-10). "Be ready when he returns by staying on guard" (*1 Peter* 5:6-8). "You were born because that's God's word that He gave to Adam and Eve. Be fruitful and multiply, and so did all of God's creation" (*Genesis* 3:14-24). "The two important dates in your life are outlined in *Job* 13:13-14: the day you were born, and the day you figure out why you were born.

"Everyone has a gift from God" (*1 Corinthians* 7:7). "Once you know what your gifts and your purpose, move quickly to build on that purpose" (*Numbers* 21:7-9; *Luke* 19:11-27). "Do something with your talent. Pay God for all" (1 Chronicles 23-30). "God's word can cancel out evil (Heb. 4:12).

"Jesus' disciple walked on the water, and as long as his disciple kept his eyes on Jesus, he walked on the water" (*Matthew* 14:23-30). Keep your sails set for on your direction as to where you want to go. (You are the captain of your ship.) One ship drives east; another drives west with the same wind that blows. It is the way you set the sail and not the gales that tell you the way to go. Like the winds of the sea are the way of fate as we voyage along through life, it is the set of a heart that decides its goal and not the calm or the strife.

"Remember, when you follow your God-given vision and talent, God has your back" (*Isaiah* 52:12; *Psalm* 121:3). "When you trust in Jesus, He will bless you, and all you have to do is pay him with thanksgiving" (*1 Chronicles* 23:30). "Amen!"

Mr. John added, "Entertain strangers" (*Hebrews* 13:2). "Moses stretched out his rod toward Heaven and Egypt was dark for three days" (*Exodus* 10:22). "Lazarus was dead and buried" in the heart of the earth of three days" (*John* 11:43).

Sign of the Times

CHAPTER 6

SIGN OF THE TIMES

Section 1

Reverend Linsey was a World War ll veteran. After serving his country, he became a farmer. Then he heard the calling of the Spirit to be a minister. He knew that God had brought him through some close calls in the war. He made it through because of his faith in the Heavenly Father. Years later, he decided to give back to the community by sharing his knowledge and experiences. So, he put a notice on the church's bulletin board announcing the subject, time, and place for various classes he decided to teach after church services. Most often, these classes would be held outside the church under the weeping willow trees. The classes would always start with just a few children, but it would end with a small congregation. The first children who came were Pieman, Charlie, and Jack just to name a few and many others joined the class.

"Hello, you all!" said, Reverend Linsey.

"Hello, Reverend Linsey!" all the children said.

Reverend Linsey began, "Today, we will talk about the signs of the times."

Pieman said, look at all those beautiful trees. This time of year, they have many colors. Why is that Reverend Linsey?

"Yes," said Reverend Linsey. "Those trees are a sign of the times. A sign of the times is an indication of something judged to indicate the nature of a particular period; the time it takes for something to grow or to go away. Like yourselves. You come into the world as a baby. You grow up get older and then you go to live with Jesus if you have been fruitful in GOD'S service. All things are based on time; or it takes time to develop. It took six days for God to make the earth, plus one day for rest" (*Genesis* 1:2). (Okay when a chicken lay an egg, through a process it will hatch a little chick or biddies, the biddies grow up into a chicken. The chicken grows up and end up on your dinner table, this is the end for the chicken because it has fulfilled its purpose in life. Now when your purpose is fulfilled in life you will go to live with the Lord, provide that you are a believer in the Lord.

Reverend Linsey added, "Things that are seen are temporal: things that are not seen are eternal" (*2 Corinthians* 4:18). "The change of seasons occurs every three months at around the twenty-first of the month, starting at the twenty-first of December–about when Jesus was born. Every three months, we get a sign of the times from God and all living beings will respond or suffer the consequences. For example, if you do not harvest your food during the autumn harvest season, you will probably miss some meals during the winter.

Reverend Linsey explained, "You can also pray to God to give you a sign on a decision you need to make. Depending on your faith, it could happen instantly, or it could take three days" (*John* 4:47–52). "Life is a process, so don't lose focus.

When you can put the physical man aside and fast or sacrifice, you get amazing results" (*2 Corinthians* 4:16). "If you fast or sacrifice for three days, you will really get spiritually strong. Jesus was in the heart of the earth for three days" (*Matthew* 27:63). Jonah was in the whale's belly for three days" (*Matthew* 12:38-40). "Jesus' parents forgot him at the feast in Jerusalem for a day's journey and had to go back and find him" (*Luke* 2:43-52). (Note to the reader: So, do not leave the Lord behind. Keep him with you always.) "When you are a God-believing servant and you miss a sign, God will contact you through another tongue or person" (*Isaiah* 28:1-3; *Genesis* 37:9, 41:15). "So, this means that you must be sober and vigilant" (*1 Peter* 5:6-8). "No water means no substance" (*Hebrews* 11-1).

Charlie asked, "What does that mean, a well without water?"

Reverend Linsey replied, "God-believing people must have faith. Faith is the substance of things hoped for, the evidence of things not seen" (*Hebrews* 11:1). "While praying and waiting on your sign, beware: Satan is present" (*Ephesians* 6:11-16). "Just remember, God's word can clear the way for you" (Isaiah 55:11; Hebrews 4:12). "Use the God-given power vested in you to make Satan flee for a season. Believers are given the power" (*Luke* 10:18-19).

Reverend Linsey said, "Remember, the water in the well symbolizes life and fertility." (Numbers 5:15-18). "So, if you do not have faith, your well have no water and you need to get a life; do something constructive."

Section 2

Some weeks later, Reverend Linsey had another gathering, and the same three children were there first for the discussion and learning.

"Good morning, Reverend Linsey!" said the children.

"Good morning to all of you!" said Reverend Linsey.

Reverend Linsey said, "Today, we will continue talking about the signs of the times. I want everybody to look around and see God's creation. Now, look at each other and see how time has been bad or good to you. Here is another way to look at it: Yesterday is history, tomorrow is a mystery, and today is a gift; that is why we call it the present. And what do we say when we get a present? We say, 'Thank you, Lord Jesus'" (*Ephesians* 5:20).

Jack said, "Yes, thank him like our Bible tells us to do" (*1 Chronicles* 23:30).

Reverend Linsey continued, "The fact of the matter is, God is everything, and everything is God's" (*Romans* 11:36; *Genesis* 1–2). "God made the whole world based on the same principle: to reproduce. Everything was created to multiply and produce more of its kind" (*Genesis* 1:27–29). "However, it takes time for this process. It takes nine months for a baby to be produced, two years for an elephant, and a mosquito can be produced in twenty-four hours. Every vegetation has its own seed, and every process takes its allotted time. This is especially true for man developing a relationship with God and thereby growing in the Spirit, attaining wisdom, and understanding" (*Proverbs* 9:10).

"Always praise God. The birds sing praise to God early in the morning. The Chickens cackle, Cow's moo. Frogs and crickets have their sounds of praise" (*1 Chronicles* 23:30; *1*

Thessalonians 3:9). "Have ye never read, out of the mouth of babes and suckling thou has perfected praise?" (*Matthew* 21:16). "God reveals things to babes" (Matthew 11:25). "The signs of the times are important for both trees and men to grow and bear fruit. A good tree brings not forth corrupt fruit, and a corrupt tree brings not forth good fruit" (*Luke* 6:43). "This means that we know who you are by the company you keep. It is so true that the environment you create determines the product you produce."

Reverend Lindsey continued, "Now, sow the seeds in a prepared place. The seeds are the word of God" (Isaiah 55:11; *Hebrews* 4:12). "Remember, a wise man gets advice from people of good judgement before making a decision" (*Proverbs* 11:14).

Section 3

About a week later, Reverend Linsey held another gathering to further the enlighten the young people about life's journey and what one can do to enhance their lives.

Reverend Linsey said, "Good evening to all of you."

"Good evening!" the children said.

Reverend Linsey said, "This evening we will talk about life's journey."

Charlie said, "Now that we are on life's journey, how does that work?"

Reverend Linsey said, "Okay, we must understand two important dates: the day you were born and the day you figure out why you were born" (*Job* 14:13-14). "In other words, when you discover your gifts from God, that's when the process starts—the signs of the times begin" (*1 Corinthians* 7:7). What are the signs of the times?"

"I'll tell you," Reverend Linsey said. "We learned that a process is a series of steps to be taken in order to achieve a particular outcome or end" (Romans 1:17).

By the age of twelve or earlier," Reverend Linsey said, continuing, "self-care routines should begin to develop: spiritual, physical, and intellectual. During this time of a person's maturing, one learns how to relate to others. Remember you are and the tools you have in your arsenal (Matthew 10:16; *Luke* 10:18-19; *1 Peter* 5:6-8; *Philippians* 4:6; *Psalm* 37:4).

"Now, to move forward, develop a passion for your gift. Work hard and you will be rewarded" (*2 Chronicles.* 15:7). "Be ready" (*1 Peter* 5:6-8). Then you might have to take the fight to the devil" (*Ephesians* 6:14-17). In this fight, you need to be ready for battle" (Isaiah 59:17, 55:11). "Beware of temptation" (1 John 2:16). "Stay close to God and pay him daily" (1 *Chronicle*s 23:30) "Now you are ready to dig some ditches to catch some blessings" (*2 Kings* 3:10-20).

Charlie asked, "What kind of ditches?"

Reverend Linsey continued, "Let me make it clear. You prepare for better future by being ready for opportunities when they are presented to you. This is referred to as preparing your own situation to be ready to catch future blessings" (*2 Kings* 3:10-20) Develop a motto for yourself. Give yourself a gift, so aim high. Believe in God and yourself. Use your brain. Be ready to go. Never quit. Expect to win. The devil is out there. Do not let him distract you. When opportunity knocks, do not be like Rhoda. Open the door" (*Acts* 12:12-16). "Remember, time waits for no one, so move quickly when the Holy Spirit puts something on your mind" (*Acts* 16:17-35).

SIGN OF THE TIMES

Sign of the Times

Section 4

Mr. Yancy was a beloved Sunday School teacher, deacon, and treasurer in the church. He had lived through the Great Depression and was known by all, so he decided to share his experience with young people wherever he found them. If Mr. Yancy saw a group of young people or children as he passed by on his way to the country store, he would tarry for a moment and say, "Hello, how are you all doing today?" Then the children would start asking him questions.

"Hello Mr. Yancy!" said the children.

"Hello, Samuel, Ray and Judy! How are you, today?"

"We are all blessed, thanks to God."

Samuel said, "My dad informed me that you were full of wisdom Could you explain what we see with a spiritual connection?"

Mr. Yancy said, "Look around at God's creation and tell me what you see, Samuel."

Samuel first looked around, then spotted some ants on the ground and asked, "What are those ants doing? They are terribly busy going and coming."

Mr. Yancy explained, "Those ants are preparing for predictable circumstances" (*Proverbs* 6:6–11). "They are created with an instinct of self-preservation which is the law of the land. Every man and creature are created with a proper gift" (*1 Corinthians* 7:7). "Ant teamwork makes dreams work. The same principle works for men. They are running all over, one behind the other. It is set on their hearts what they must do, so they move quickly" (*Philippians* 3:14).

Samuel said, "I see now. They would work extremely hard in good weather and chill during bad weather. So, we should work hard so we will get good grades in the future."

Ray said, "I can work outside when the weather is good and make me some pocket change for when the weather is not so favorable."

Judy replied, "I will work hard at everything that I do. That way, I will have more choices of what I can do."

Mr. Yancy said, "You are all so right, and I am so proud of you all because you understand so well. The ants are moving quickly, and the reward will be given every creature according to his work. Rewards are based on the work we do (*Revelation* 22:12).

"When you disturb the work of the ants, they will come after you with a vengeance. "When you disturb those little creatures, they bring the fight to you as a team" (*Ephesians*.

6:14–17). "If one bites you, they have won because the Creator has their back" (*Isaiah* 2:12).

Ray shared his observation, "I think the way they are running one behind the other is teamwork, and teamwork makes dreams work."

Judy said, "Yes, it is like a dream when they work so good together."

Mr. Yancy said, "The ants are clothed in natural protection. When you disturb the ants, they attack with vengeance" (*Isaiah* 59:17). "You could learn from ant ethics. You have to realize that you can't change a man's morals, but you can adjust his attitude."

Note: This is truly a sign of the times, that time is a non-expendable resource that everything is based upon. Time brought all into the world and the evidence is the sign that time takes all away. Once time is gone, it is gone. So, learn the valuable lesson from the ants and how they heed the signs of time. Once time is gone, it is gone.

This is the Way

CHAPTER 7

THIS IS THE WAY

Section 1

Mr. Yancy was a God-fearing man and a farmer, and he loved to invest in young people. He would always say, "We must pass all the knowledge/wisdom on so as to educate our young men and women." Knowing how to build a family is paramount in our lives. That is the bedrock and foundation of making a house a home. It was observed throughout the community that when he talked to the families, they would make better decisions in their personal matters, especially with their children. Mr. Yancy met with Bill and his wife Lady, who is blind.

Mr. Yancy greeted the couple. "How are you today?

Bill replied, "We are truly blessed. How are you, Mr. Yancy?"

Mr. Yancy said, "I am blessed also! Last week we talked about life's paths and how we walked in them. In the future, you will need to know all you can about life, everything your parents told you about the old path, when the parents had more influence on their children's lives. If you have knowledge of the past, it will give you knowledge for the future because history always repeats itself" (*Jeremiah* 6:16; *Proverbs* 1:8-9). "When you have a family with children, expose them to God's house so they can get God's word" (*Matthew* 5:13). "Remember, in order for you to be a good leader, you must be a good follower of your parents' instructions or follow the spirit you saw in your parents' spirit" (Proverbs 1:8-9). Then your young ones will recognize the spirit of almighty God, who is omnipotent, which means having all power, omniscient, meaning having all knowledge, and omnipresent, meaning everywhere at the same time" (Ubiquitous) (*Revelation* 19:6; *1 Corinthians* 2:10; *Psalm* 137:7-10).

Bill said, "This tells us that God is everywhere that we are" (*1 Corinthians* 9:19-25).

"Yes", Mr. Yancy said, "he is always there on the spiritual line of communication between you and God, and you can ask God what you want with faith" (*Hebrews* 11:1). "Yes, He is there, especially when you prepare a habitation for him" (*Exodus* 15:1-2; *1 Corinthians Cor.* 9:19). The line is open spiritual communication between you and God.

Bill asked, "What are the effect of these guidelines?"

Mr. Yancy replied, "The atmosphere you create will determine the product you produce. The time and effort you put into something will always show in the product, which will determine the product and personalities you produce in the land of the living. *Psalm* 51:10 shows David asking the Lord to create a clean heart and spirit within him. Remember, newborns desire the sincere milk of the Word (salt) that they may grow thereby" (*Matthew* 5:13; *2 Peter* 2:2).

Bill said, "When they are young, it's the best time to grow in the spirit.

"Yes," Mr. Yancy agreed. "Now we will talk about your vision for the family that you desire" (*Joel* 2:28). "You have this vision of having a family. A vision will motivate you enough to act coherently with focus and determination over a long span of time. Along with your vision, you will encounter spiritual warfare. (*Ephesians* 6:11-14). "Now you are in the arena with opportunity and opposition. When you overcome opposition, the only thing left is your opportunity" (*Ephesians* 6:13). "May you be blessed for following your parents' instructions, the old path" (*Proverbs* 1:8-9; *Jeremiah* 6:16). "Your parents did tell you to prepare for Him (God) a habitation" (*Exodus* 15:2). "Now you can call on Him because you trust in God's word" (*Isaiah* 55:11). "On this spiritual journey you are among wolves" (*Matthew* 10:16). "However, you have God's protection" (*Luke* 10:18-19). "Memorize some Bible verses like Psalm 64:3, and *1 Peter* 5:6-8, *1 Timothy* 6:19, *Ephesians* 5:20, *Proverbs* 3:6, and *Hebrews* 9:15.

"Our basic Christian life is based on believing that Jesus was crucified, dead and buried for three days then God raised him" (*1 Corinthians* 15:4; *Luke* 23:6-7; *Romans* 10:9).

"Here are some basic rules to follow," said Mr. Yancy. "Believers get more power to plead for God's mercy" (*Acts* 17:3). "Always confess your sins and restore your relationship with God. Build up the good things you do" (*1 Timothy* 6:9). "Master your time, then master your life. When God's children pray for something, He will normally answer in three days if you do not ask amiss" (*James* 4:3; *Matthew* 12:40; *John* 11:43-44; *Exodus* 8:27, 15:22-26; *1 Kings* 20:5).

Mr. Yancy added, "Delight in the Lord and he will give you the desire of your heart" (*Psalm* 37:4).

Section 2

Mr. Yancy met with the family again at the church because some other young people heard about the meeting and wanted to join Mr. Bill's family for the meeting. Now, due to time restraints, only Bill and Lady could ask questions.

"You all look terrific," Mr. Yancy began. "How are you today?"

Bill and Lady said, "We are still blessed with God's grace."

Mr. Yancy said, "Yes, we are being blessed. Today, we will talk about salt and compare its function with God's words. Remember, salt is used in the purification process of water. Salt, in its natural form, is a crystalline substance. When light shines upon a crystal, it reflects light, sometimes to an area that has less light. We also know that the moon has no light of its own, but it reflects the light of the sun upon the earth at night, especially around the time of the Passover."

Note for the reader: The moon was full on the night of the Passover so the destroyer would see the lamb's blood and pass over that house (*Exodus* 12:21-27).

Mrs. Lady asked, "Mr. Yancy, can you clarify please?"

Mr. Yancy replied, "Sure. This means that God made two great lights, the greater light, one rules the day and the lesser light rules the night. The moon only reflects the greater light. Similarly, people will follow the light they see in you" (*Romans* 2:15). "God is the sun. The Lord said, 'A long as I am in the world, I am the light of the world'" (*John* 12:46). "I am come to bring light into the world and whosoever believeth on me should not abide in darkness" (*John* 12-46). "Your body is the temple of the Holy Ghost, which is in you" (*1 Corinthians* 6:19). "Some men love darkness rather than light because their deeds are evil" (*John* 3:19). "Now you have the spiritual blessings in your arsenal to go forth in life and fulfill your vision. You are prepared for this, when you become aware that the Holy Spirit has been awakened within you. So, now you can see things with natural sight and spiritual/mental sight" (*Joel* 2:28). "This is the way to fulfill the reason why you were born" (*Romans* 12:3). "You must pay God daily and nightly" (*1 Thessalonians* 5:17; *Philippians* 1:4; *Daniel* 6:10; *Ephesians* 5:20; *1 Chronicles* 23:30). "This will get you ready to take the fight to the devil" (*Isaiah* 59:17). "Since the devil likes to operate in darkness, sprinkle some salt, meaning God's word, on him. The salt crystals reflect the light as the moon reflects the light from the sun. Our Lord is the light of the world" (*John* 9:5). So, the Passover is formed with God's word which is the light and the marking on the doorpost is salt (God instructions and word) and the evil one that abide in darkness can not survive in the light nor the reflection of light because it will expose them. Evil cannot stand the light of God's word.

Bill asked, "What will he do then?"

Mr. Yancy continued, "When you sprinkle him with the salt of God's word, he will flee for a season because the word is too much light since Satan that like to work in darkness." (*Luke* 4:13). "Be aware; he will return" (*Ephesians* 6:13). "Submit yourself to God (*James* 4:7).

"Since you are a believer in the Lord, you have asked for a sign of things to come. He will respond to your request. Now the Holy Spirit will speak in thine ears and you shall hear words behind you saying, "This is the way, walk ye in it" (*Isaiah* 30:21). "If you ignore your conscience, that will later render it inoperative" (*Romans.* 2:15). "So, follow your heart and not your eyes. Protect your heart (*Job* 31:7; *Proverbs* 4:23).

"Jesus spake again unto them saying, 'I am the light of the world. He that follows me shall not walk in darkness but shall have the light of life'" (*John* 8:12). "The Lord's word is a lamp to my feet and a light unto my path" (*Psalm* 119:105). "Evil casts out evil" (*Matthew* 12:26).

Mr. Yancy told them, "Watch and pray that ye enter not into temptation, the spirit is willing, but the flesh is weak" (*Matthew* 26:41). "Be not forgetful to entertain strangers: for thereby some have entertained angels unaware" (*Hebrews* 13:2; *Matthew* 6:9).

Section 3

Mr. Yancy met with Bill and Lady again with some other church members. This time, it is on Saturday morning. Mr. Bill and Lady and others were invited to ask questions during this session. (This session was at the Church.)

Mr. Yancy said, "Good morning, my brothers and sisters" (*Matthew* 12:50; Mark 3:35).

"Good morning, Mr. Yancy," Bill, Lady, Joel, and others replied.

Mr. Yancy asked, "Did you all pay God yet for today?" (*Ephesians* 5:20; *1 Chronicles* 23:30).

Mr. Yancy said a prayer. After his prayer, Mrs. Lady's heart was touched. She was so moved by Mr. Yancy's prayer that she asked God, "Direct me, Lord! I am blind, but I believe in your grace. (*1 Corinthians* 15:10).

Mr. Yancy said, "So, now you get the day off to a great start. In all your ways acknowledge him and he shall direct your path" (*Proverbs* 3:6). "We were born in sin with both good and bad in us" (*Genesis* 3:5; 2:17). "So, you have a choice: going to hell, or everlasting life" (*Daniel* 12:2). "Now, before it's too late, ask the Lord to give you a sign to help you in your decision-making process" (2 *Chronicles* 32:22-33).

Joel asked, "How do we get these signs, by praying for them?"

Mr. Yancy responded, "God made everything with its signs. When it is going to rain, the clouds come. Changes in the season show signs: winter, spring, summer, and autumn. So, you can also ask the Lord for a sign for different things that come in your life" (2 *Samuel* 5:24). "Remember, when you sacrifice to be in prayer with God, he will definitely hear and answer your request. For example: you do not go for a drink at the club. Instead, give the Lord that time, praying for the sign you want. Once you have prayed for your sign, then you must be sober and vigilant; the devil may try to devour you" (*1 Peter* 5:6-8). "If you just say, 'Jesus' aloud, the devil will leave you for a season" (*Luke* 4:13).

Bill said, "So, when we say, 'Jesus,' that's salt?" (*Matthew* 5:13).

"Yes," Mr. Yancy answered. "The son of God lives in the human body" (*Exodus* 25:8). "That's Jesus' tabernacle, which means dwelling place" (*Exodus* 23:20-21). "So, when you acknowledge him through your sacrifice, He will direct your path" (*Proverbs* 3:6). "Then your ear shall hear words behind you saying, 'This is the way, walk ye in it" (*Isaiah* 30:21). "You hear him behind you because he has your back" (*Isaiah* 52:12). "Also, don't forget to entertain strangers" (*Hebrews* 13:2).

Mr. Yancy continued by saying, "Life is a constant war against the spirits" (*Ephesians* 6:11-13). "When you accept the Lord as your savior, he will guard you with your sign that you ask for and day night God will not slumber" (*Psalm* 121:3). "God will not overload you" (*1 Corinthians* 10:13). "God will protect you in many ways if you keep paying him" (*Ephesians* 5:20). "If you observe signs that you ask for, your conscience speaks to you, especially when it's decision time. Remember, if you ignore your conscience too many times it will become inoperative" (*Romans* 2:15).

Bill said, "I get strength just watching and listening to you, Mr. Yancy."

Mr. Yancy continued, "That's wonderful. People often follow the spirit they see in others" (*Romans* 8:9). "Teach your children to help each other" (*Galatians* 6:2-3). "When you trust in God, sprinkle the salt of His word all about, causing the souls of men to thirst for living water" (*Matthew* 5:13; *Jeremiah* 17:13). "When God prepares the way and sends angels before you, nothing can hinder your blessings" (*Exodus* 20:33). "He will even let you know what person to see" (*1 Kings* 17:9). "Then you can say, 'I am walking in victory because I know who I am'" (*1 Corinthians* 15:10).

Section 4

Mr. Yancy met the group again. Mr. Yancy said a prayer, then greeted the group. This Friday evening, he noticed that the group had increased, and since this was a Friday evening, he knew that the people were sacrificing some time for God to get into their hearts.

"Good evening! Good to see you," Mr. Yancy said.

They all said, "Good evening, Mr. Yancy!"

Mr. Yancy said, "We will discuss receiving blessings this evening. One of the main ways to receive blessing is to thank God, starting with the Lord's example in *Matthew* 6:9. Acknowledge him in all thy ways and he will direct thy path" (*Proverbs* 3:6). "And delight yourself in God and get the desires of your heart" (*Psalm* 37:4).

Mr. Yancy continued, "Now that you are saved and have wisdom and understanding, it is time to make sure that your children are exposed to the challenge of seeking God on a higher level by sacrificing time to God. Encourage your children to help each other" (*Leviticus* 16:6). "Then, He will dwell as He promised" (*Exodus* 33:14). "God desires to transform our bodies into His Holy Temple by means of a new birth" (*John* 14:23). Then, the young believer can be exposed to the true light" (*John* 1:6-9, 8:12). "We should reflect the light of God's word in dark, sinful places" (*John* 3:19; *1 Corinthians* 6:19). "The Lord will not change; He is the same today, yesterday, and forevermore" (*Hebrews* 3:8; *Revelation* 1:8). "Since Christ won't change, follow the old Christian path" (*Jeremiah* 6:16).

Bill said, "We must give our young clear instructions.

Mr. Yancy replied, "That is true, because what you tell them stays with them for life" (*Proverbs*1:8-9). "Continue to sprinkle the salt of God's word on them" (*Matthew* 3:13; *Isaiah* 55:11; *Hebrews* 4:12). "And when you ask the Lord to direct you, you will hear a voice saying, 'This is the way, walk ye in it'" (*Proverbs* 3:6; *Isaiah* 30:21). Everyone will not hear a voice, but you will see or hear the sigh you ask for.

Bill stated, "When you stray from God, He will bring you back home."

Mr. Yancy agreed, adding, "As your faith increases, you will experience spiritual events. An example is Cornelius, a devout believer in the Lord" (*Acts* 10). "Sometimes, you will know when you are straying away from God, then you have to go back where you left Him" (*Luke* 2:43-52). "Faith is a powerful weapon that you have in your spiritual arsenal because it results in a vision of what God can do" (*Hebrews*11:1; *Romans* 1:17). "The vision will motivate you to act coherently with focus over a long period of time.

"Don't forget to thank God for this vision. Do not be like some people. Christ healed many, but only one of this group came back to thank Jesus" (*Luke* 17:15-19). "Always give thanks to God (*Ephesians* 5:20). "When you serve God with your whole heart, sacrifice, fast, and pray" (*Mark* 9:25-29; *James* 4:6; *1 Corinthians* 15:10).

Ms. Lady asked, "How can you check your faith?"

"Well," said Mr. Yancy, "If life gives you a lemon, let us put some water and sugar with it and make some lemonade. When you have a life situation and someone really gets on your nerves, pray on it with your whole heart, then speak with that person the next day, putting some of God's words into the conversation as salt, and you will acknowledge that the Master was involved because the person changes their attitude" (*Hebrews* 4:12). "Pray for one of your friends who is in the need of prayer, then ask them the next day how they feel" (*Matthew* 8:1-13).

Ms. Lady asked, "And faith?"

Mr. Yancy continued, "Put your faith and trust in the Lord and He will fight your battle" (*Isaiah* 37:36). "Now be alert. Because you asked God to direct your path according to Proverbs 3:6, you will hear a voice, which is your conscience, saying, 'This is the way, walk ye in it'" (*Isaiah* 30:21). "Remember, faith is the substance of things hoped for and the evidence of things not seen" (*Hebrews* 11:1). "Delight yourself in the Lord and He will give you the desire of your heart" (*Psalm* 37:4). "All you need is as much faith as a mustard seed" (*Luke* 17:6). "Always close your conversation with God's word" (*Hebrews* 4:12; *Isaiah* 55:11). "Job's friends had faith when the Spirit told them to go and let Job pray for them" (*Job* 42). "They followed the instructions of the Spirit, Job followed the instructions of the Spirit, and Job was blessed with more than he had before. When you exercise your faith, you can honestly say, 'By the grace of God I am what I am'" (*1 Corinthians* 15:10).

Section 5

Mr. Yancy met with the group again on a Saturday morning the next week at the church.

"Good morning, Mr. Yancy," they said together.

"Good Morning," said Mr. Yancy. Then he said a prayer for the small group.

"This morning, we are going to talk about some guidelines you can give to your offspring."

Ms. Lady asked, "Mr. Yancy, you have enormous wisdom and understanding. What should I pass it on to my offspring?"

Mr. Yancy said, "Start them with finding Jesus." First learn the Lord's prayer. (*Matthews* 6:9-) (*Romans* 10:9; *1 Corinthians* 15:4). "Make sure that your children understand the power of God's word" (*Isaiah* 55:11; *Hebrews* 4:12). Embed within your children a desire to help each other, the strong helping the weak" (*Romans* 15:1; *1 Corinthians* 15:4). "They must know that God gave them gifts to do what He wants them to do" (*Romans* 12:3-12). "Teach your child to look at the tangible and the intangible with two kinds of sight" (*2 Kings* 6:14-17). "Be aware, sometimes the devil will be subtle in his approach" (*Genesis* 3:1). So, you see, when you have prepared a habitation for God in the spirit of your mind, then you should sprinkle some salt on those around you right away" (*Exodus* 15:1-21; *Ephesians* 4:23). "Keep God's word in your mind" (*Matthew* 5:13). "God will speak to them in their dreams" (*Joel* 33:14-17).

SEASONING FOR THE WORLD

Bill asked, "How can I tell if my child has a gift?" (*1 Corinthians* 7:7).

Mr. Yancy responded, "When they pray for help with their decision-making, get out your Bible and open it. Most of the time, you will find your answer on that page. If not, keep reading for a paragraph. Keep your eyes open for your child's interest. If they are doing something that they want to do more than they want to eat, that's usually an indicator of the talent they've been gifted with" (*1 Corinthians* 7:7; *Philippians* 3:14). When you see that God has given your child a talent, encourage them to move quickly and build on that talent" (*Acts* 12:7). "Encourage them to continue praying without ceasing and get a full understanding of their talent" (*1 Thessalonians* 6:16-17). "Remember the signs you ask for" (*2 Samuel* 5:23-24).

Mr. Yancy continued, "Encourage them to set aside time for prayer. People often follow the God they see in the lives of others, so set the example and they will follow" (*Romans* 2:15). "God will send an angel before you" (*Exodus* 33:2).

Mr. Yancy responded, "God is faithful; He will not suffer you to be tempted above what you are able to bear, but with the temptation will also make a way to escape, that ye may be able to bear it" (*1 Corinthians* 10:13). "God does not slumber" (*Psalm* 121:3). "God moves at midnight" (*Acts* 12:1-18; *Matthew* 25:1-30).

Mr. Yancy continued, "Raising children is like growing wheat. While you are doing your best to raise the wheat, someone may come along at night and throw tares in your wheat field" (*Matthew* 13:18-49). "In our lives, we have the bakers of *Hosea* 7:4. Don't try to snatch up the tares by the roots; you will damage the wheat. You just keep sprinkling God word (salt) on the tares and it will stunt their growth and strengthen your young ones, who are considered the wheat."

Mr. Bill, remembering what Mr. Yancy had said before, added, "Prepare for a miracle" if you want a miracle" (*2 Kings* 3:10-20).

Mr. Yancy continued by asking them a question, "How do you make God happy?" (*1 Thessalonians* 5:16-17). "First, confess your sins and put your faith in Him" (*Acts* 3:19; *Hebrews* 11:1). "Second, establish a communication link in your mind. Third, pray and watch" (Philem. 1:16). "Never ask God amiss for your own lusts" (*James* 4:3). "Always praise God."

Section 6

Mr. Yancy says, "Okay, let us take this down to a point so a blind person can see it clearly. You can see this when you focus with your mind in a spiritual sense. First, they must believe" (*Romans* 10:8-9, *1 Corinthians* 15:4).

Ms. Lady asked, "How is a blind person going to see this?

Mr. Yancy continued, "One must understand that creation functions the same way as a garden and produces products through a process of osmosis that balances the creation, and all grows toward the sun. So, when we prepare for sowing the seeds, we remove large debris" (*Matthew 13:3-9, 18-40*). "When you are ready for your young ones to grow spiritually, you must create the environment so they can grow thereby, and that will determine the product or personalities you produce" (*Matthew* 13:31-32). "Are you with me? Now give them the salt of God's word" (John 1:1; *Matthew* 5:13).

Mr. Bill and Ms. Lady replied, "Yes, sir."

Mr. Yancy continued, "Now teach them about leaning on faith to navigate this journey." (*Hebrews* 11:1; *1 Thessalonians* 5:17). "Preparation continues through life. The word of the Lord endures forever" (*1 Peter* 1:25). "Now, when you sow your wheat (children), an evil one could come by at midnight and throw tares into their lives" (*Matthew* 13:18-40).

Ms. Lady said, "That's very clear!"

Mr. Yancy continued, "We know that God does not slumber" (*Psalm* 121:3). "The wheat is not afraid of the tares. Your children, they will sprinkle the salt of God's word on the enemy, meaning the tares, and pray" (*Matthew* 5:13; *John* 1:1; *1 Chron.* 23:30). "Ask God to direct their paths" (*Proverbs* 3:6).

Mr. Yancy continued, "The tares in your lives are like the baker in (*Hosea* 7:1-7). Now, as your young ones grow, teach them how to make God happy" (*1 Thessalonians* 5:16-17). "Have faith in God" (*Hebrews*11:1). "Now let's teach them to walk on water and move mountains" (*Mark* 6:49, 4:31; (*Matthew 17:20, 13:31; Luke 17:6, 13:19*). "All this comes about through faith in God" (*Hebrews* 11:1). "Your young ones followed the godliness they saw in you, and now the other children will follow the godliness they see in your children. The birds in (*Matthew* 13:31-32) refers to other children who will nest in their mustard bushes; a blind man can see that. Let them know that they are one of God's soldiers, fighting the evil ones with the salt of God's word, which will make the evil ones destroy each other" (*2 Chronicles* 10:20-25). "You see, the singers went out before the army singing and praising God's holiness and that won the battle. Commit (*Hebrews* 4:12 and *Isaiah* 55:11) to memory. Growing in God is a source of strength for many generations as your children teach their own children" (*Isaiah* 11:1-16; *Matthew*

28:20; *Hebrews* 13:8). "Teach them that when they are planted in God's house, they will still flourish in their old age" (*Psalm* 92:13-15). "In real life, tares are the enemy—like wolves" (Luke 10:18-19, *Matthew* 10:16).

Mr. Yancy continued, "God is everything and everything is God" (*Genesis* 1). "Do not do something just because; evaluate first. When your child speaks to a bully with God's word, tell them do not be afraid of their faces" (*Jeremiah* 1:8-9; Isaiah 52:12). "Have compassion on the bully" (Luke 15:20). Tell the bully his mind is the table for his heart (*Proverbs* 3:3).

"Remember, bullies are like the tares" (Hosea 7:1-7). Do not forget, even though you are among wolves" (Matthew 10:16). "Do not forget that you have God's word and that He is protecting you" (*Isaiah* 55:11; *Hebrews* 4:12). "All you need to do is use His word and have faith in Him" (Hebrews 11:1). "So, do not be a well without water (substance). Have faith! Then, pray without ceasing" (*1 Thessalonians* 5:17). The water in one is well is an indication of life and fertility. This means that you are not a busybody" (1 Timothy 5:13).

Mr. Joel asked, "How do we handle this?"

Mr. Yancy clarified, "When you pray, it makes you ready for battle and you can take the fight to the devil" (*Ephesians* 6:14-17). "Put on the whole armor of God" (*Eph.* 6:13; *Isa.* 59:17). "When you fight with God's word, God will supply all your need according to his riches in glory by Jesus Christ from His unlimited resources" (Phil. 4:19).

"Understand how your vision works" (*Romans* 1:17). "God will not overload you" (1 Corinthians 10:13). "But by the grace of God I am what I am" (*1 Corinthians* Cor. 15:10).

Section 7

One Saturday evening outside under the weeping willow tree, Mr. Yancy said a prayer for the group, then greeted them. Mr. Yancy would pray first go dispel any evilness of hearts.

"Good evening, Mr. Bill and Ms. Lady," he said.

They replied, "Good evening, Mr. Yancy."

Mr. Yancy said, "Sometimes, life will be a little boring. What do you do in a situation like that?"

Ms. Lady said, "We go for a walk or to a singing concert."

Bill said, "Well, we can go for a walk through a flower store or garden store so we can smell the fragrances together."

Mr. Yancy agreed and gave them additional ideas. "You can also sharpen your skills on your God-given talent, and not just let it lay in memories gone by. Cultivate ideas. Discuss and refine family goals and plans, focusing on the family's objectives."

Bill added, "We can do hobbies together."

Mr. Yancy continued, "Yes, all of those are great ideas. Now, how about practicing and honing your skills and your God-given talents, such as singing, playing a musical instrument, or writing songs?" (*1 Corinthians* 7:7; *Romans* 12:3). "During trying times, you must be creative to maintain your sanity and not be a burden on each other. You see, when you make yourself ready, God will help you" (*John* 4:34; *1 Corinthians* 10:13). "David always practiced with his sling while watching his sheep and became king as a result of his practicing his talent with the sling" (*1 Samuel* 17:1–58). "Plus, David was a man after God's own heart" (*Acts* 13:22). "Allow opportunity to walk in. One must condition themselves to listen to their heart and the Spirit. So, before you go to bed nightly, pray the prayer in *Proverbs* 6:22."

Mr. Yancy said, "You should share this information with your children and grandchildren so that when they are bored, they will know what to do. When they get into a situation, they can reflect on *Proverbs* 1:8-9. God will love that you are teaching others the way to Him. Understand that if you never give a child or person this information, they will not have it to remember when they need it. Even if they do not remember it verbatim, they will have a starting point to build on. Learn at least one Christian song. God loves music and praise.

"Learn how to listen to the Spirit. Then, when you wake the next day, listen to the Spirit even before you get out of bed. The Spirit will give you answers on what you must do in succession" (*Acts* 16:8-9). "Being a Christian, life is a growing adventure" (*Romans* 4:20). "At some point, you will notice people starting to follow the godliness they see in your life" (*Romans* 2:15). "With God in your plan, you will always bounce back.

"Always thank our Almighty God for 'creating love that can start more fires than hate can put out'" (*Genesis* 17:1; *1 Chronicles* 23:30; *1 Thessalonians* 5:16-17

Mr. Yancy continued, "Learn all you can about every good thing you can. Sometimes, you cannot go forward because you have forgotten where you have been. Do not be an empty wagon that makes a lot of noise. Remember, change your thinking and you will change your life. Now be of good courage. God is wherever you are. (1 Corinthians 9:19-25) Never forget. The environment that you create will determine the personalities or product you produce. Create an environment that is good for human development for spiritual, physical, mentally, emotionally, and socially. This balance will help your young ones to meet their full potential. Then give them some responsibility (Read about David, his father gave him responsibility. (1Samuel 17: 34-) Amen!"

CPSIA information can be obtained
at www.ICGtesting.com
Printed in the USA
LVHW030330200721
693166LV00002B/252